# Dancing in Sunlight

## DR. DIANA PRINCE

AuthorHouse™
1663 Liberty Drive
Bloomington, IN 47403
www.authorhouse.com
Phone: 1 (800) 839-8640

The cover and the interior photos are used with permission of Getty Images.

This book is printed on acid-free paper.

ISBN: 978-1-7283-2282-7 (sc)
ISBN: 978-1-7283-2283-4 (hc)
ISBN: 978-1-7283-2281-0 (e)

Library of Congress Control Number: 2019911651

Print information available on the last page.

Published by AuthorHouse 08/09/2019

authorHOUSE®

# TABLE OF CONTENTS

# MERMAID

I dreamed I was a mermaid
Beneath the sparkling sea,
And when I sat upon a rock,
The children waved to me.

The fishes were my little friends,
And they came swimming by,
In that most perfect place I lived
Between the earth and sky.

We spent our mornings singing
And sitting in the sun,
And looked for pirate treasure
Before the day was done.

We lived each day to leap and dive,
And everything was so alive,

And like the other mermaid girls,
My hair was long and full of curls.

# RUNNING THROUGH THE FIELD

Down through the tall green grass,
We ran that day,
As dragonflies dipped down
along our way.

Laughing as we went
down little trails,
That closed behind us
like a grassy veil.

The grass was fresh and green and new,
And barely touched
by morning's early dew,

It was so special,
I can now recall,
And you were there with me
to share it all.

# EASTER BUNNY VISIT

The Easter Bunny left us eggs
Along the garden fence,
And inside the old flower pot.
We haven't seen him since.

My Mom insists she saw him
Hopping among the flowers,
But I was tucked away in bed;
I'm sure it took him hours.

My sister promised she'd stay up
To catch him unaware,
But she was sound asleep
When he left eggs upon the stairs.

And on the parlor table,
There was much more than that—
He left a chocolate bunny
With a bowtie and a hat.

# GETTING UP EARLY

Now spring is here,
I wake up early—
long before the bees.

Already waking birds outside
Are singing in the leaves.

That little girls awake so soon—
no one really supposes.

Outside I find the butterflies
are sleeping in the roses.

# LIVING IN TREES

How nice to have a home in trees,
And to confer with honeybees,
Who also make their homes so high,
And have a window to the sky.

To huddle under leaves in rain,
Then watch the sun come out again.
To hear the winds come whistling by
And watch a rainbow fill the sky.

To be a giant looking down,
and feel leaves flutter all around,
To be the one to greet and sing
hello to robins in the spring.

# DANCING IN SUNLIGHT

In spring the whole world dances.
Trees sway to heaven's height.

Night falls away. Each day we rise
like birds lift into light.

And something magic happens
When spring is in the air,

And from the hidden shadows
Bluebells are everywhere.

When winter goes away to sleep
And tucks itself away,

The sweet peas curl their perfect blooms
Into each perfect day.

And nothing is impossible
Or out of reach somewhere

When spring is back and here to stay,
And finally in the air.

I am a pinwheel whirling,
the far-off church bell ringing.

And spring becomes the perfect song
You never can stop singing.

# THE MOUSE IN SCHOOL

Johnny brought a mouse to school,
Although it was against the rules.
He said for "share time" we could see
This mouse could dance and even read.

We sat around his box entranced—
He did not read. He didn't dance.
But best was when the mouse got out
And chased the screaming girls about.

# FLYING MY KITE

Flying my kite on a windy day,
Above the waters of the bay,
I wonder if on a distant shore,
Someone sees my kite from the other side.

Does some child in another land
Feel the tug of his own kite in his hand,
As the string stretches out and rises high,
And his kite, like mine, climbs against the sky?

# PICKING WILDFLOWERS

The first day of spring
We hop out of bed,

Forget about chores,
Grab our baskets instead,

And run to the hillside
With Mary and Flo,
Down where the bluebells
and buttercups grow.

And hardest of all
is having to choose,
When the flowers surround us
in yellows and blues.

Here's one for my mother,
Here's one for my doll,

And a daisy to put
in the vase by the hall.

# WHEN AUTUMN COMES

When Autumn comes
The leaves spin down,
And cover grass
Without a sound.

When autumn comes
Wind blows our hair,
And bright red leaves
Are everywhere.

When Autumn comes,
We run outside
To where
Our little puppy hides—

Leaves in his fur,
Bright orange and red.
We play until
It's time for bed.

# PICKING APPLES

I picked them out,
Each shiny one,
And held them to the morning sun.

Each one of them so red and new,
And dropped them in my little sack.

Clouds followed me
And traced my tracks,
And watched me pick the biggest ones,
And finally I headed back.

Mom saw me from the kitchen door,
And on the porch Dad smoked his pipe,

When I brought apples home that day,
And all of them so ripe!

# RAIN BOOTS

I like to wear my rubber boots
and squish them in the grass,
And splash through puddles on the street
as sleek and clear as glass.

I walk through puddles in my boots
After the summer storm,
And all the while, my little feet
inside are safe and warm.

# THE PILOT

When I grow up, I'll fly a plane,
Where mountaintops rise steep and still,
Or columns press against the sky
In ancient temples on a hill.

I'll fly over the jungle green
of Africa and circle free,
And wave to all the children there,
Who run outside to wave to me.

And on the way to other lands
Where mighty pyramids stand tall,
I'll circle in my silver plane
Over the Sphinx to see it all.

The world is such a special place,
So many people short and tall,
Each one a friend I've yet to meet;
I know someday I'll meet them all.

# AT THE PARK WITH MOM

We must have walked past every tree,
The leaves flew up into the air.
With every step, and every breath,
The flying leaves were everywhere.

Roads disappeared beneath our shoes,
A leafy blanket filled the street,
And old familiar paths
Just disappeared beneath our feet.

# AN AFTERNOON WITH DOLLS

It was a lovely sunny day—
I lined up all my dolls to play.

And I was quite surprised to see
How very busy dolls can be.

My dolly Betty sat alone,
Just talking on her little phone.

And Ruthie sat inside the nook
And would not leave her story book.

Sweet Ann leaned on the windowsill
And watched the robins on the hill.

But Dolly Sue sat down with me
For cookies and a cup of tea.

# MARBLES EVERYWHERE

Out of the sack, marbles rolled out,
Like planets scattered all about.

Across the polished floor they flew
In little swirls of green and blue.

And Mom's stern face told us at last,
We'd better pick them up, and *fast*.

There must have been a hundred there
Along the walls, under the chairs,

We got them all, and stopped to rest.
I think I like the "Cat's Eyes" best.

# TAKING KITTY FOR A WALK

My yellow boots are on my feet
To walk the rainy morning streets.

My coat is zipped
To keep me warm,
And safe and sound
Out in the storm.

I hear my little kitty purr,
All cozy in her coat of fur.
She wants to go with me to town,
With all the raindrops pouring down.

And when the sun appears outside,
Kitty is walking by my side.

And minus shoes, and coat and hat,
She's warm and cozy
      Just like that.

# TOY TRAIN

The locomotive hums along
And travels down the track.
The coal cars follow close behind,
And oil tanks in back.

Along the track, the houses sit
With people all about.
There is a little park with trees,
And benches all laid out.

We cross a bridge over a lake
And travel on so fast,
The little children wave at us,
As we go speeding past.

And we ride through the tunnel
So high above the ground,
And then I am the engineer,
And king of all the town.

# THE SNOWMAN

I love when snow comes sifting down
and covers everything around,

And then I run with Dave and Bill
to build a snowman on the hill.

We get a shirt from Dad's old clothes,
and find a carrot for his nose.

And if he's the distinguished type,
We might get him a scarf and pipe.

No matter what we try to do,
He only stays a day or two.

# BEACH CASTLE

Bucketful by bucketful
I fill this little hole with sand,
And soon my little castle here
Will be magnificent and grand.

The beach goes on forever here,
And here the moat will run,
And lovely ladies dressed in silk
Will glitter in the sun.

# AUNT GENEVA

Whenever Aunt Geneva's here
We must be quiet in the house,
And walk on tiptoe everywhere,
And be as quiet as a mouse.

Sometimes she even falls asleep,
And though we close the doors,
It sounds just like a storm comes through
when Aunt Geneva snores.

# SATURDAY

My sister is making a dress for her doll,
My brother is reading a book down the hall.

My Dad is washing his car in the drive;
My Mom is still waiting for mail to arrive.

And even the dog at the end of the hall
Is playing and chasing after the ball.

And I am just sitting with nothing to do
On this Saturday morning at quarter-to-two.

# FOREST WALK

Into the magic forest
We slipped away one day,

The trees swayed all about us
In a fluttering of leaves,

From somewhere little ladybugs
Climbed blossoms and hung on,
They held on upside down, and then,
They suddenly were gone.

And whirring came the dragonfly—
A blur of wings in flight,

He hovered near and hung midair,
He didn't want to leave,

And then he fluttered near again,
and landed on my sleeve.

The bluebells bent their small heads down
As if they were asleep.

And by the brook I even
Picked some maple leaves to keep.

And in one tree, the bees buzzed round
Their little honey towers.

We must have walked for hours that day
Among the magic flowers.

# PET TURTLE

Our turtle is a puzzle,
As far as I can tell.
Some days he simply disappears
And hides inside his shell.

Sometimes he listens carefully,
To everything he's heard,
Or pulls his head inside his shell,
And doesn't hear a word.

It really is a little rude,
And happens every day.
And never does he ever
Have a single word to say.

# NATIVITY SCENE

Each year we get the boxes out
And set the figures all about.

We place the three kings in a line
And wrap their little gifts with twine.

The shepherds come and put their sheep
Next to the place where Jesus sleeps.

So if the night might rain or storm,
The sheep will keep the Baby warm.

And most of all before we stop,
The angel always goes on top,

And hovers there with wings unfurled
To bring His message to the world.

# LITTLE SWIMMER

Well, all my friends
are splashing here
in Jonathan's big pool,

I can't be sure what I like best
this first day out of school.

The books are closed and put away,
with no cloud anywhere,
And when we dive, the pool's alive
With flowing mermaid hair.

It is the perfect kind of day
To jump and run and splash,
And far as I can tell,

It is lots better than a bath!

Printed in the United States
By Bookmasters